Kona

Haunted Hele

Guidebook

Mahalo!

By Zach Royer

Author of the Hawaii Vortex Field Guide

COPYRIGHT INFORMATION

An imprint of Kahuna Research Group

10 9 8 7 6 5 4 3 2 1

Also from KRG Publishing

<u>Maui Vortex Field Guide</u>
(Zach Royer, 2019. Also available on Kindle)

<u>Hawaii Vortex Field Guide</u>
(Zach Royer, 2014. Also available on Kindle)

<u>Apocalyptic Revelations: The Emergence of Earth's Spiritual Awakening</u>
(Sean McCleary, 2019)

<u>Black Robe: The Kempo/Kajukenbo Connection</u>
(David Tavares, 2017)

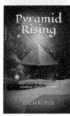

<u>Pyramid Rising: Planetary Acupuncture to Combat Climate Change</u>
(Zach Royer, 2012. Also available on Kindle)

BIG ISLAND GHOST TOURS

DEDICATION

This guidebook is dedicated to the late Glen Grant, who is most likely still leading ghost tours somewhere…

Aloha & Mahalo.

CONTENTS

* Places marked with an asterisk have
an informational plaque on site or
nearby.

BIG ISLAND GHOST TOURS

ACKNOWLEDGMENTS

Akua. God. Great Spirit. Prime Creator. Thank You. No words can convey the amount of thanks and gratitude I feel on a day to day basis while on this incredible journey of life and, most assuredly, death.

Such is the life of a paranormal investigator.

My thanks also go out to all the ghost tour operators and paranormal enthusiasts across the world. Because of you, the history and mystery of human culture is kept alive and fresh in the minds of the present day people, the stories we talk about continuing to inspire folks from beyond the veil of time and space.

Mahalo nui,
Zach Royer

HAWAII'S PARANORMAL
BACKGROUND

Hawaii Island is called the "Big Island" because it is larger than all the others combined. Many mystical stories on the island tell of Pele, the volcano goddess, or of the feared Night Marchers. A local once told me that Pele occasionally takes on human form, either as an old woman accompanied by a small white dog, or as a tall young woman of striking beauty. He said if you encounter her it is essential to be kind. Other native Hawaiians I spoke with were certain Pele exists, with stories of her presence going back thousands of years to the dawn of creation.

In Hawaii, it's a common belief that the uhane (oo-ha-nay), or human soul, leaves your body at night and wanders around in search of knowledge, experience, or adventure, returning only when you wake up. When you die, it travels to the leina (lay-ee-nah), sites believed to be portals to the Other World. Sometimes, the uhane gets lost on the way, or the ancestral guides do not come and it remains as a wandering spirit on earth.

Death in old Hawaii, particularly the death of a high chief, was not an event to be taken lightly. In mourning, relatives and close friends would weep copiously, and chant to eulogize the deceased. They might hack away their hair close to the sides of their head leaving only a crest down the middle, knock out a front incisor with a stick or stone, scar their skin with burning twigs, or in rare cases, even cut off an ear. Reverend William Ellis, in the early 1800s, wrote of seeing Queen Kamamalu endure great pain while having a line tattooed on her tongue after the death of her husband, Liholiho. When Ellis asked her about the pain, she responded, "The pain is indeed great, but the pain of my grief is greater."

For at least two thousand years, native Hawaiians have placed the earthly remains and spirits of their "kupuna," or ancestors, within the landscapes. Remains of high chiefs or those kupuna of high honor often were interred at night to conceal their location from jealous rivals who might steal, degrade or otherwise use the spiritual power of the remains for personal gain.

Because of these cultural practices, ancestral bones can be found almost anywhere in Hawaii today. It is important to never disturb any graves or ancient sites you may come across. Burial sites are often accidentally disturbed either by nature (high surf or erosion) or by human activity through projects that involve excavation. Construction on top of more ancient ruins is a common occurrence throughout the world. Nearly every building here in Kona was built on or near burial grounds, ancient settlements or temples of worship. There just aren't that many places to keep building when you live on an island like this.

Archaeological features and historic sites once covered much of the Kailua to Keauhou section of the Kona Coast. With the urbanization of the area, this pattern has changed. Historic preservation laws did not come into place until the early 1970s. Development prior to that time was focused in the core of Kailua Village and mostly seaward of Ali`i Drive. This development proceeded without archaeological survey and many historic sites were destroyed in these years, with records being only brief survey work. Since the early 1970s, most developments have been preceded by archaeological surveys, and in the late 1980s, these increased in number and quality with a resurgence of development. Only a few areas in Kailua Village lack survey at this point.

Corpses were treated with respectful ceremony in preparation for internment, as it was believed the bones, the iwi, of the dead held great mana, divine power, that contributed to the natural order of life, and could benefit whoever possessed his ancestor's bones. Burial caves have been found on every Hawaiian Island. Because of these cultural practices, ancestral bones can be found almost anywhere in Hawaii today.

Unfortunately, by the time many of the caves were catalogued by authorities, they had already been discovered and looted. Most chiefly families are believed to have had their own secret burial caves, the location of which was closely guarded by the kahu, or family retainer. Sometimes stone walls that looked like the surrounding cliffs were cleverly constructed to hide a cave entrance.

Remains of bodies uncovered in the last century have revealed a variety of burial methods, depending on the island and on whether the deceased was a commoner maka'ainana; or royalty, Ali'i. The skull, leg, and sometimes the arm bones of kings, in particular, were preserved, hidden or guarded. Hawaiian historian David Malo left written descriptions of the bodies of Ali'i being wrapped in banana, taro and paper mulberry leaves, and then buried in shallow graves in the shrine area of the men's eating house. While a priest chanted, fire burned over the body for ten days. The body was exhumed, and the flesh and soft parts were peeled away and deposited in the sea. The remaining skull and long bones were wrapped in tapa and arranged in a sitting position on a shrine. While the priest prayed, the dead king was believed to transform into a god.

The town of Kailua-Kona was officially established in 1812 by King Kamehameha I to serve as his seat of government, which I explain in detail a bit further in this book. The king, originally a chief of Kona, unified many of the Hawaiian islands through years of armed conflict and he needed a central location from which to govern, his compound at Kamakahonu in Kona being a natural choice. In this way, Kailua-Kona became the first capitol of the Kingdom of Hawaii. Later it would be moved to Lahaina on Maui and eventually Honululu on Oahu, which is still Hawaii's capitol today. The town later functioned as a retreat for the Hawaiian royal family.

Up until the late 1900s, Kailua-Kona was primarily a small fishing village. In the late 20th and early 21st centuries the region underwent a real estate and construction boom fueled by tourism and investment. Growth and development of the Big Island over the years has transformed many sections of the island to what it is today. During this progress, sacred grounds were desecrated and buildings were built on top of ancient burial grounds. Though steps were taken to culturally preserve sacred areas, disturbance did take place, which is one of the most common reasons for paranormal activity to occur.

START LOCATION:
HOTEL BANYAN TREE

The most prominent and evident tree near the King Kamehameha Kona Beach Resort and the Kailua Pier is an Indian banyan tree. Planted over 100 years ago, this tree marks the start location of the Kona Haunted Hele ghost tour.

Originally from a cutting that was a gift from Indian royalty given to King Kalākaua, the tree was transplanted to its current location more than 100 years ago after not thriving at its previous location on a private ranch, and Queen Kapiolani was said to have planted the sister banyan tree at Hulihe'e Palace in the late 1800's.

No trees are home to a more motley mix of supernatural creatures than the banyan tree whose eerie aerial roots are adept at seizing imaginations in their grip. Diverse cultures around the world say these trees shelter angels and fairies, gods and ancestral spirits, ghosts and other malevolent creatures.

There may be a biological basis to some of these beliefs. Banyan trees attract ghostly nocturnal animals such as rats, leathery-winged bats and small primates with big eyes that reflect moonlight. In Indonesia and Malaysia, these trees are often home to small saucer-eyed primates called tarsiers (Tarsius tarsier) whose local names mean 'spirit animal' or 'spirit monkey'.

Other denizens of banyan trees are decidedly less cuddly. In the folklore of the Philippines, they include giant tree demons called kapres, goblin-like duendes and the half-human, half-horse tikbalang.

On the Japanese island of Okinawa, folk tales feature impish red-haired spirits called kijimuna that live inside the hollows of banyan trees. These mischievous sprites love to play tricks on passing people, such as sitting on their chests so they can't breathe.

In Australia, Aboriginal stories warn of an altogether more fearsome fig-dweller, the yara-ma-yha-who. This man-like creature has bulging eyes and a gaping toothless maw. When hungry it will leap out of its fig tree onto an unsuspecting traveller. Its fingers and toes end in flattened discs, through which it sucks the blood of its victims.

These are just a few of the many supernatural beings that people across Africa, Asia, South America and the Pacific say live in fig trees. Whether ancient people realized it or not, by protecting banyan trees, they were ensuring the survival of many other species of plants and animals upon which they depended. That's because banyan trees are ecological linchpins. They produce figs year-round, sustaining a rich variety of birds and mammals that disperse the seeds of many other forest species. Without banyan trees many of these animal and plant species would simply go extinct.

Although the banyan is an alien species to the islands, it has managed to find a comfortable home in Hawaii, and is now woven into the fabric of modern Hawaiian history and landscape. So the next time you see a banyan tree, fear not. The world would be a scarier place without them!

SITE 1:

KAILUA PIER*

The historic Kailua Pier covers a turtle-shaped rock that may have inspired early Hawaiians to name the small bay just north of the pier, Kamakahonu (lit.: the eye of the turtle). The extended rock outcropping later gained distinction as the "Plymouth Rock of Hawai`i," acknowledging the site where the first Christian missionaries landed in Kona on April 4, 1820.

Originally the pier was built to facilitate loading cattle onto steam freighters bound for Honolulu. Before the advent of the pier, horseback cowboys used to rope and drag individual steers from Kaiakeakua Beach (the minuscule beach just south of the pier), plunge them into the surf and swim them out to waiting whaleboats. There, the cows were lashed to the gunwales of the whaleboat and, with their backs awash, ferried farther out to the steamer offshore. The cows were then, unceremoniously, by means of sling and crane hoisted aboard the steamer.

The pier has been a focal point for two world-famous events. The Hawaiian International Billfish Tournament (HIBT) first launched at the pier in 1959, is known around the world as the "grandfather of all big-game fishing tournaments." Each afternoon during the tournament, spectators gather to watch the big-fish weigh-in. The pier also serves as the start, finish, and bike transition area for the Ironman World Triathlon Championship, first held in 1981. Each October more than 7,000 resident and visitor volunteers help the more than 1,800 triathletes, and the pier is one of the best places to catch the excitement throughout the day. The November 2015 Dengue fever outbreak on the Big Island is thought to have originated from someone visiting during October 2015 Ironman.

Kamakahonu is on the register of National Historic Landmarks as one of the most important historical sites in Hawaii, and at least eight major historical events happened here to corroborate such a claim:

1. Pa o 'Umi - This is near the site where 'Umi-a-Līloa, a fifteenth century paramount chief, came ashore and set up a new royal center after leaving his ancestral court at Waipio valley. He was a ruling ali'i-ai-moku (district high chief of Hawaii) who inherited religious authority of Hawaii from his father, High Chief Liloa, whose line is traced unbroken to Hawaiian "creation".

2. It was the final resting home of King

Kamehameha I. This is where, during the early morning hours of May 8, 1819, at the age of 82, King Kamehameha transitioned to the next life.

3. In 1812, seven years before his passing, the King established the area as the piko, or center, of political power, much like the capital city of any US state, giving it the name Kailua-Kona.

4. The first Christian missionaries from New England were granted permission to come ashore here on April 4, 1820, less than one year after the death of the King Kamehameha I.

5. King Kamehameha's son, Liholiho, was educated here for his role as future king. A few months after the passing of his father, he broke the ancient kapu system by dining with women, effectively ending the system that began many centuries prior.

6. It was here that John Adams Kuakini resided as the governor of the island before building Hulihe'e Palace.

7. It was also here that the young prince Le-le-I-hoku II enjoyed the calm of Kona before his death.

8. King Kalākaua maintained a residence and made a boathouse out of a historic building here.

While Kailua Village had served as the capital of Hawai`i after Kamehameha I united the islands and up until his death in 1819, by the time the small pier was built the village had become a sleepy backwater. That is with the exception of "Steamer Day," when the pier became the focus of activity as inter-island ships laid anchor in the bay. Schools would close and everyone came into town to meet visitors, pick up their mail and supplies, and catch the latest news. A visitor to Kailua Village in 1898 describes the pier as the place to get "figs or grapes wrapped in their own leaves," and to "pry out the secrets of the town," while "cheerfully munching."

In several places along the seawall, if you look 20-60 feet offshore, you will observe the distinct "boil" associated with undersea fresh water springs discharging into the ocean. These springs result from the discharge of aquifers that collect fresh water far up the mountain slopes and transport it down to where they intersect the seafloor. Ancient Hawaiians used to dive under the surface of the ocean with a sealed gourd, down to the springs, turn the gourd mouth-end down, uncork it and fill the gourd with fresh water. This was a necessary task to obtain fresh water, as fresh water springs are scarce in the Kona district. Today, one can often spot honu (sea turtle) languorously swimming through the springs, trying to kill parasites and algae that grow on their shells and skin.

Even many locals will be surprised to learn that the tiny beach adjacent to, and south of, the pier and the little beach associated with Hulihe'e Palace both have names; respectively they are Kaiakeakua (the god of the sea) and Niumalu ("in the shade of the coconut trees") Beaches. Snorkeling from Kamakahonu, Kaiakeakua or Niumalu beaches is spectacular and strangely uncommon. A beautiful coral garden and abundant fish are to be seen snorkeling along the shoreline of Ahu'ena Heiau and fish, turtles, moray eels and the occasional sunken boat are abundant in Kailua Bay.

SITE 2:
AHU'ENA HEIAU*

Ahu'ena translates to "altar of fire", "red hot heap", or "burning altar" depending who you ask, and is known as a place of alignment to the sun and the sun's energy, perhaps the reason for the name. The site is of extreme significance to the Hawaiian people, both in ancient times and modern. It is what you would call a "chosen place". When the sun first peeks over Hualalai Mountain, its initial rays touch ground at Ahu'ena. The ancient name for the site of this heiau was Kalake'e, which means a "Place of Light". The Hawaiians and the kupuna, the teachers, understood these alignments well. This solar surprise was recently confirmed by a resident who was at the area during the sunrise.

This alignment is imperative to the Hawaiian people who were much attuned to nature and the heavens, believing they originally came from the stars, specifically the Pleiades constellation, of which they base the start of the Makahiki festival on. Once this constellation touches the horizon, a time of peace ensues, and it was during this peace time when Captain Cook first "discovered" the islands.

After uniting the Hawaiian kingdom, King

14

Kamehameha the Great returned from Oahu to Historic Kailua Village in 1812 to rule from his compound at Kamakahonu. Here, he could see the vast upslope crops known as the Kona Field System as well as the strategic positioning of Kailua Bay.

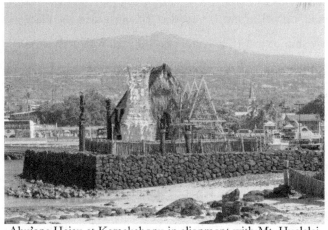

Ahu'ena Heiau at Kamakahonu in alignment with Mt. Hualalai.

Many descriptions and illustrations of the impressive Ahu'ena Heiau, the religious temple that served Kamehameha, were done by early voyagers. The distinctive anu'u (oracle tower) indicated a heiau of ruling chiefs. As Kamehameha rose to power, Ahu'ena was deemed among the most powerful heiau of the island of Hawai'i. Ahu'ena Heiau served his seat of government as he ruled the Kingdom of Hawai'i.

Shortly after returning from Oahu, the king ordered the pre-existing heiau remodeled and renamed as Ahu'ena Heiau, a temple of peace and prosperity dedicated to the fertility god Lono. After the King's son Liholiho abolished kapu, Kamakahonu went through several other changes. The wall around the compound was enlarged and built up, 'Ahu'ena Heiau was changed from a place of worship to a fort, and the sea wall was widened. In 1820, Liholiho moved the Kingdom's capital from the Island of Hawaii to Lahaina on the Island of Maui. He appointed Kuakini, who was Queen Ka'ahumanu's brother, governor of the Island of Hawaii, and Kamakahonu continued to be the capital for the island. Kuakini built a two-story wood frame house and a school for the *ali'i* in the compound. Kamehameha I's bones were quietly removed from the *hale poki* in the 1820s and hidden and the *hale poki* fell into disrepair. In 1837, Kuakini moved to Hulihee House further east along Kailua Bay and Kamakahonu was used for government offices and ceremonies.

Before King Kamehameha I remodeled this heiau in 1812 to what it presently looks like, a special type of heaitu was here, called a **luakini**, existing at this spot for centuries is accordance with the ancient kapu system. This luakini heiau was dedicated to the war god Kukailimoku. In ancient Hawaii, a luakini was a sacred place where human and animal blood sacrifices were offered. In Hawaiian tradition, luakini heiaus were first established by Pa'ao, a legendary priest credited with establishing many of the rites and symbols typical of the stratified high chieftainships of the immediate pre-European-contact period.

This heiau was also King Kamehameha I personal temple, where he communicated with the gods. It was where he transition to the next life in a stone hale named that was nearby on the beach named "Ka Hale Pua Ilima" - "The house of the Ilima flower" - in 1819. He died at the age of 82 from an inflamed cyst (kuapuhi) on the back of his neck, nearly one year before Christians arrived in Kona in 1820. His final words to Chief Ka Lani Moku before his passing were: "*E na'i wale no oukou I ku'u pono, aole e pau.*" "Strive as ye may to undo the good that I have accomplished, ye shall never reach the end." as noted by sketch artist Henry Kekahuna on his sketch of the house as it existed in 1950.

King Ka-mehameha I's Last Words
It was in this house that the king uttered his last Prophetic words to Chief Ka-la'ni-moku:
"E na'i wale no oukou I ku'u Pono, aole e Pau"
Strive as ye may to undo the good that I have accomplished, ye shall never Reach the end.

He knew the end of the kapu system was on the horizon and he spent his entire life trying to preserve the ancient ways which ultimately died with him. The end of the kapu system kicked off a mission to burn down every heiau in Hawaii, led by Queen Kaahumanu and Kamehameha II. A few still remain today, some of which have been restored, such as Ahu'ena heiau, while others are slowing breaking down over time.

BATTLE OF KUAMO'O

The year following the death of Kamehameha I in 1819 was a turbulent time for Hawaiians. The Native community was divided by the abolishment of the kapu system by Liholiho (Kamehameha II) and Kamehameha I's wife Kaahumanu. Shortly after the king's death, Hawaiian forces clashed over the traditional kapu religious system in the battle of Kuamo'o . The dispute pitted the forces of Kekuaokalani, nephew of Kamehameha I, who sought to preserve the traditional system, against his cousin, Liholiho (Kamehameha II), who had abandoned the kapu system. Liholiho was victorious, but many warriors from both sides perished in battle and were buried on the property, including Kekuaokalani and his wife, Chiefess Manono. With her dying breath, Chiefess Manono is said to have uttered "Mālama kō aloha"- "keep your love"- a plea to both sides that no matter what obstacles come to Hawaii, keep your love of one another.

Accounts of the historic battle and the events leading up to it differ. In general, before Kamehameha I died in May 1819, he named two heirs – his son Liholiho (Kamehameha II) received his lands and political power, and his nephew Kekuaokalani was entrusted with the care of his feathered war god Kūkāʻilimoku. Strongly encouraged by Kamehameha I's powerful queens/widows, Keōpūolani and Kaʻahumanu, Liholiho symbolically shared a meal of forbidden foods with the women of his court to set aside the kapu and initiated ʻai noa, eating without restrictions, but meaning a time of no adherence to the traditional Hawaiian religion, laws, and regulations.

Historian Samuel M. Kamakau wrote that the time of mourning a beloved aliʻi nui was the time to ʻai noa, and that when the period of mourning was complete, the new ruler would reestablish the kapu and reset the order of the kingdom. So, it is possible that the meal shared by Liholiho and the women of his court was observed in a time of traditional ʻai noa, and Liholiho chose not to reinstate the ʻai kapu. Regardless, either the breaking of the ʻai kapu, or Liholiho's choice to not reinstate the kapu was a drastic change. Liholiho's cousin, Kekuaokalani, resisted this change. In December 1819, Liholiho sent his Prime Minister Kalanimoku to defeat Kekuaokalani and the forces he had amassed.

Kekuaokalani marched up the Kona coast from Ka'awaloa and met Kalanimoku's forces at Lekeleke, south of Keauhou. The battle was fought with muskets, spears, slingstones and clubs. Kalanimoku's/Liholiho's forces were supported by a swivel gun mounted on a double hulled canoe and cannons on a western frigate. The first skirmish is said to have favored Kekuaokalani – with Liholiho's forces suffering a temporary defeat at Lekeleke. Liholiho's forces regrouped and allegedly trapped Kekuaokalani at Kuamo'o between forces on land and a flotilla of canoes at sea. Kekekuokalani's wife Chiefess Manono (sister of Kalanimoku) accompanied Kekuaokalani into battle, and was slain beside him at battle's end. Thousands of warriors died, along with the ancient traditional belief system that existed unchanged for many centuries. Liholiho ordered that his men be buried in the terraced graves at Lekeleke, located to the north of the property. Kekuaokalani, Manono, and their followers are said to have been left exposed or buried at Kuamoʻo under makeshift stone cairns.

The Battle of Kuamoʻo marked a pivotal turning point in Hawaiian history. Following the battle, traditional gods were abandoned and kiʻi representing those gods destroyed. Historian Kamakau interpreted the Battle as the fulfillment of the prophecy of the famous seer Kapihe – who told Kamehameha that the islands would unite, the taboos will fall, the high shall be brought low, and the low shall rise to the heavens. Others disagree with Kamakau and feel that the prophecy has yet to be fulfilled. The rest of the Traditionalist followers of the old religion dispersed to the protection of the four High Chiefs of the Big Island of Hawaii who sponsored the Traditionalist rebellion. They were ultimately pardoned.

Within a year, American Christian Protestant Missionaries such as Asa Thurston and Hiram Bingham arrived, and the culture was forever changed. There has not been a battle of that size on the island since. The establishment of a new religious system here was the underlying cause of many untimely deaths. Ancient warriors fought to keep the traditional beliefs in place, and they ultimately paid with their life. Modern religion, as well as modern weaponry, beat out the ancient Hawaiian beliefs, making Hawaii what it is today.

In addition to this historic and pivotal battle, the land at Kuamoʻo includes Lonohelemua Heiau and Pūʻoʻa Heiau, shrines and ceremonial areas, sea caves (haunt of the shark-god Ukanipo), salt pans, agricultural terraces, the remains of an historic village and residence, and part of the Ala Kahakai National Historic Trail. You can get there by following Aliʻi Drive to the southern end, turning right at the Keahou light intersection and another right on the access road. There is a marker on-site to commemorate the lives lost.

On a more positive note, a portion of all sales from our tours and books goes towards preservation of these ancient sites, such as Ahuʻena and Kuamoʻo , so a big MAHALO for your support!

SITE 3:

KING KAMEHAMEHA
KONA BEACH HOTEL

Urban legend, as well as eye witness reports from employees, says that the top floor of this hotel is haunted. People have reported hearing footsteps, chanting, and battle cries or smelling a distinct flowery perfume along the corridors. Some witnesses even claim seeing ancient Hawaiian warrior apparitions.

The reason for this alleged haunting seems to be in the fact that this area is where King Kamehameha lived out the end of his life. Local legend says his bones are buried somewhere near or under this hotel, but some in-depth researching shows that is not the case. When Kamehameha died May 8, 1819, his body was hidden by his trusted friends in the ancient custom called hūnākele (literally, "to hide in secret") mainly because the mana, or power of a person, was considered to be sacred. As per the ancient custom, his body was buried hidden and his final resting place remains unknown.

King David Kalākaua, an avid historian and fellow author, had also once attempted to search for Kamehameha's lost bones. He found a man named Kapalu who supposedly knew where King Kamehameha's bones were buried. Kapalu said that the cave that houses Kamehameha's bones was called Kahikuokamoku (sometimes called Kahiku Okalani); this cave is supposedly located in the Kaloko-Honokōhau complex. Kalākaua found two bundles of bones, one supposedly belonging to Kamehameha and the other claimed to be the bones of 'Umi-a-Liloa. Kalākaua had the bones taken to O'ahu in the February of 1888, then, years later, Dr. Louis Sullivan of the American Museum of Natural History, examined both sets of bones, and concluded that neither set was of Kamehameha. Though, there is a theory that Kalākaua actually found Kamehameha's bones, but kept his discovery secret.

According to the curator of the Royal Mausoleum of Hawai'i, a direct descendant of Hoapili and Ho'olulu, Kamehameha's bones are concealed in a cave off the coast of Kona on the island of Hawaiilocated right off the shore of the old residence of 'Umi-a-Liloa, which is supposedly in the hands of the QLCC (Queen Liliuokalani Children's Center) Trust. At one point in his reign Kamehameha III asked that Hoapili show him where his father's bones were buried, but on the way there Hoapili knew that they were being followed, so he turned around.

Again, the exact location is a secret and only known

only by his descendants which is really how it should be. The Big Island is dotted with burial caves, the disturbance of which is what is most likely the cause of the paranormal activity here...

HAUNTED OIL PAINTINGS

According to a popular website that collects supernatural stories from the Hawaiian islands, the last picture at the far left of the gallery in the hotel is a portrait of Queen Liliuokalani which is said to be haunted. According to the report, the unsmiling picture appears to breathe in and out while glaring at you. I have been to the gallery many times and never experienced anything unusual but that doesn't mean the reports aren't true.

TSUNAMI BONES

On March 11, 2011, Japan was hit with a disastrous 9.0 earthquake followed by a series of large aftershocks. The following day, Hawaii was hit with a tsunami that was generated as a result of the large earthquake, and I happened to be in Kona at the time and experienced the tsunami first hand. Fortunately, no one was seriously injured but many businesses suffered catastrophic damage.

At King Kamehameha's Kona Beach Hotel, the tsunami wreaked havoc, flooding the property's entire first floor and bursting into waterfront shops, sending broken glass, sand and debris everywhere. The hotel's restaurant, which faces the ocean, was hit especially hard. All totaled, the King Kamehameha suffered seven million dollars in damage.

What many people don't know about the tsunami and the debris it left behind is that after the water receded from the hotel it was discovered that two full human skeletons had washed ashore and into the hotel. It is believed that the skeletons were sacrificial victims of the kapu system and buried under the hotel beach or just offshore, a common practice of ancient times. The bones were reinterred in a new burial heiau behind the hotel in an inconspicuous spot so as to not drawn any unnecessary attention from guests, complete with its own "kapu" sign.

SITE 4:
HULIHE'E PALACE

Built out of lava rock and coral in 1838 by Governor James Kuakini, the palace was also used for many years by Hawaiian royalty as a summer get-away and a place of great galas and parties. When Kuakini died in 1844 he left it to his hānai (adopted) son William Pitt Leleiohoku I, the son of Prime Minister William Pitt Kalanimoku. Leleiohoku died in the measles epidemic of 1848 and left it to his son John William Pitt Kīna'u, but he died young and the palace went to his mother Princess Ruth Ke'elikōlani. Ruth made Hulihe'e her chief residence for most of her life, but she preferred to sleep in a grass hut on the palace grounds rather than in the palace. She invited all of the reigning monarchs to vacation at Hulihe'e, from Kamehameha III to Lili'uokalani. Ruth died and left the palace to her cousin and sole heir Princess Bernice Pauahi Bishop.

It was later sold to King Kalākaua and Queen Kapi'olani. Kalākaua renamed the palace Hikulani Hale, which means "House of the Seventh ruler," referring to himself, the seventh monarch of the monarchy that began with King Kamehameha I. In 1885, King Kalākaua had the palace plastered over the outside to give the building a more refined appearance. After Kalākaua's death it passed to Kapiʻolani who left Huliheʻe Palace to her two nephews, Prince Jonah Kūhiō Kalanianaʻole Piʻikoi and Prince David Kawānanakoa. For some reason, it was left to ruin in 1914 when in 1927-1928 the Daughters of Hawaiʻi, a group dedicated to preserving the cultural legacy of the Hawaiian Islands, restored Huliheʻe Palace and turned it into a museum. It was added to the National Register of Historic Places listings on the island of Hawaii in 1973 as site 73000653. If you look close you'll see the entrance gate of the Palace displays the royal Coat-of-Arms of the Hawaiian monarchy.

It is said that the spirits of the Hawaiian monarchs still inhabit this palace, walking up and down the grand staircase and around the grounds on occasion.

According to a local resident, they walked in to the palace one day to discover more about their Hawaiian ancestry, and they had a ghost sighting. According to the sighting report, they were at the bottom of the staircase and something told them to look up, and when they did they saw the half-bodied apparition of Princess Ka'iulani, one of the palace's tenants for many years, wearing a white dress and descending down the steps in a royal manner. A few steps away from the man she disappeared, leaving him feeling shocked and amazed for the remainder of the day, having just connected with the spirits of the Ali'i.

Such was the case during a previous ghost tour in 2015. We were in front of the palace and I was explaining to the guests about the story of the lady in the white like I do on every tour. My back was to the palace at that time, so it was the guests that saw it first. A woman in a long white dress with dark hair appeared out of the bushes just beyond the gift shop and proceeded to stand and look out onto the ocean for at least five minutes before disappearing behind the palace. I managed to snap three photos of the supernatural encounter and will include one here so you can see it now:

Even employees at Hulihe'e palace have also reported seeing the apparition of a little Hawaiian boy, quite possibly the young Prince Albert, son of Kamehameha the fourth, who allegedly died of appendicitis after being exposed to cold water by his father's

orders in an attempt to reduce a high fever.

Former palace curator, Fanny Au Hoy, described the palace grounds as a puuhonua or a refuge in that it gives a

feeling of welcoming comfort. The mana is so special and so spiritually healthy that it creates a calm place to be. Every now and then you'll get a chicken skin moment. You know when you're being watched, but it's not a bad feeling — it's a feeling of calm. Sometimes, employees of the palace have reported, when they are at the palace alone and locking up, they can feel that sense that you're not alone.

One of the more interesting things about the Palace is the derivation of its name, Hulihe'e. Huli means "to turn or spin" and comes from the same root as "hula" the "dance of turns". He'e is a generic term for cephalopods (octopus and squid). The term "spinning octopus" refers not to an aquatic species, but rather to a form of tactical defense employed by the Hawaiians when defending coastline against superior attacking forces. The defenders are spread-out in arms, or tentacles, which rotate from area to area as waves of attackers come ashore.

Previously housed on the palace grounds was the Pōhaku Likanaka, pōhaku meaning "stone." This stone, originally located at Kahalu'u beach Park further down Ali'i Drive, was used for executions. Sacrificial victims were forced to sit in front of it while a rope was fed through the hole, around their neck, and then back through the hole. They would then be strangled... probably not a nice way to go – and probably the most likely reason for paranormal activity here.

Pōhaku Likanaka

Also on the grounds is Kiope Pond, a spring fed pond that was once the main water supply for the Palace. As a pyramid enthusiast and vortex researcher, I've learned that anytime water is forced through earth, a small electric charge is generated, usually in the form of negative ions. Is this why spirits find it easy to manifest at the Palace? Only time and testing will tell. The palace is a very beautiful, historical and energetic location, I really recommend the day tour if you get the chance!

SITE 5:

MOKUAIKAUA CHURCH*

In 1819, sent by the American Board of Commissioners for Foreign Missions, the first American Christian Missionaries set out from New England aboard the Thaddeus bound for the Big Island of Hawaii. While at sea, King Kamehameha I died and his son and successor, Kamehameha II, overthrew the Kapu system of spiritual rules and beliefs, which had been practiced for years by Native Hawaiian leaders. Hawaiian high priest Hewahewa foretold a prophecy that the new God would come to this same rock in a black box.

After 164 days at sea, the missionaries, including two ministers, two teachers, an apprentice printer, a farmer, and their spouses, finally arrived on the shores of Hawaii in 1820. The first Christian missionary that came ashore carried his Bible, protected in a black wooden box, as he stepped on the rock at Kailua pier. Many of the Ali'i royalty of Hawaii interpreted their arrival and the fulfillment of Hewahewa's prophecy as a divine sign and converted to Christianity.

King Kamehameha II and the Queen Regent Ka'ahumanu gave the missionaries permission to stay in

Hawaii and teach Christianity. They were given land near the harbor, across from Royal Governor Kuakini's Hulihe'e Palace, to build the first Christian church in Hawaii, at Kailua at Kona on the Big Island. After the royal court relocated to Honolulu, they briefly moved there. In October 1823, they learned that the people of Kailua-Kona had developed an interest in the new ways and had erected a small wooden church. The first structure on the site was made from Ohi'a wood and a thatched roof, on land obtained from Royal Governor Kuakini across the street from his Hulihe'e Palace. The name Mokuaikaua literally means "district acquired by war" in the Hawaiian language, probably after the upland forest area where the wood was obtained.

Mokuaikaua Church is the first and therefore oldest Christian church in Hawaii. In April 1820, the American Protestant missionaries who were sent to Hawaii by the American Board of Commissioners for Foreign Missions first landed here in Kailua-Kona, then the capital of the Hawaiian Kingdom.

The church congregation dates to 1820 and the current building was constructed and completed between 1835-1837. The state historic place register lists it as site 10-28-7231 as of January 1978. On October 3, 1978, it was added to the National Register of Historic Places as site number 78001015. In 2014, the National Trust for Historic Preservation included the church on its annual list of "America's Eleven Most Endangered Places" as it is at risk from both earthquake damage and natural wear and tear.

Mokuaikaua Church represents the new western architecture of early 19-century Hawaii — a combination of local Hawaiian materials and New England architecture. It is 120 feet long and 48 feet wide, and it's steeple, at 112 feet tall was once the tallest structure in town.

The exterior of the church was built with lava rocks sourced from a 15th century heiau and mortar made from sand and crushed coral, so essentially the missionaries destroyed one temple to build another, a good enough reason for any supernatural activity if you ask me. A cemetery once existed where the current parking lot is.

The interior features native Hawaiian woods. The posts and beams are made of wood from the Hawaiian ʻŌhiʻa Lehua tree and are joined together with ʻŌhiʻa pins. ʻŌhiʻa Lehua trees are usually found between elevations of 1,000 and 9,000 feet. Some sources say the ʻŌhiʻa Lehua wood used in the church's construction came from Mt. Hualālai. We saw many of these native Hawaiian trees as we explored Hawaii Volcanoes National Park. The interior wall paneling, pulpit, and pews are made of wood from the

Koa tree. The Koa tree is the largest native tree in the Hawaiian Islands reaching heights of about 115 feet. Commercially, Koa is one of the most expensive woods in the world.

The first church was destroyed by fire and in 1835 construction began on a new stone and mortar structure. The church sits today much as it did over 200 years ago when it was built. The interior is decorated with Koa wood. The church continues to be in use and is open to the public for tours, with some artifacts on display, such as a scale model of the Thaddeus. The small graveyard fronting the church is all that remains of the original cemetery and is the final resting place for some of the earliest missionaries and includes an old unmarked grave made from lava.

Meanwhile, Kamehameha I's family dynasty flourished. He died in 1819, and his first-born son succeeded him to the throne. Known as impulsive, Kamehameha II was fascinated by the foreign missionaries who had begun to come to the islands. In 1823, against his court's advice, he sailed for England with his favorite of his five wives, Kamamalu, with the goal of thanking George IV, who had sent him a ship.

The visit was unannounced, and the monarch's arrival in London was the talk of the town. The appearance and behavior of the unfamiliar couple fascinated English observers, who reported on their every movement. Though the public was enthralled by the visitors, George IV put off seeing them. "As if I would sit at the table with such a pair of damned cannibals," he said.

That biased perception of Hawaiian islanders was common among the British, who looked down on Native Hawaiians' religion and considered them to be uneducated and uncouth. By the time the king finally agreed to meet the Hawaiian delegation, Kamahameha II and Kamamalu were dead, apparent victims of measles they are thought to have contracted during a visit to the Royal Military Asylum, an orphanage for the children of military parents that was known for its epidemics of childhood diseases.

In July 1824 the Hawaiian king and queen would be disinterred from the graveyard at London's St. Martin-in-the-Fields church and put on a ship back to their home, the Hawaiian Islands (called the Sandwich Islands at the time).

Just days before their untimely death, the royals' every move had been avidly covered by the press, from Kamamalu's provocative enjoyment of cigars to Kamehameha's trip to the city's zoo and puppet theater. The interest was well warranted: The Hawaiian king and queen may have been looked down upon by George IV's court, but they were also London's most talked-about couple.

The measles deaths of Hawaii's monarchs were tragic—and foretold another tragedy. Twenty-four years later in 1848, measles and pertussis made their way to the Kingdom of Hawaii via missionaries and ships' crews, killing off a quarter of the population. Until their contact with Europeans, Hawaiians had lived in an isolation that helped their culture and population flourish. That isolation ended up contributing to their downfall. During the 19th and early 20th century, epidemics of measles, smallpox and other diseases threatened to wipe out the entire Native Hawaiian population, and disrupted the culture and lives of the island's residents. European contact didn't just change the structure of Hawaii. It also brought new diseases to the islands. Cook's crew introduced sexually transmitted diseases like syphilis and gonorrhea. Because of their island location, Native Hawaiians lacked immunity to infectious diseases like these, and they spread quickly. So did a "plague" that struck the island around 1803. Thought to have been yellow fever or a similar disease, the epidemic resulted in up to 175,000 deaths, cutting the island's pre-contact population in half.

It was just the beginning: wave after wave of infectious disease continued to hit Native Hawaiians. Since Native Hawaiians lacked any exposure to these disease at all, they were even more susceptible to even benign-seeming infections. "An illness that was considered to be relatively mild could cause severe or fatal consequences to the unprotected native population," write historians Robert C. Schmitt and Eleanor C. Nordyke. Climate, geography, and poor medical treatment exacerbated the outbreaks, they note.

"Hawaiians were an extraordinarily strong and healthy people who lived in a bubble, a kind of bubble that was a paradise in many respects," historian David Stannard told *Honolulu Magazine*. "But when that bubble was penetrated by ships laden with people who carried an armada of diseases—diseases that they themselves could live with—it destroyed the Hawaiians who simply had no defenses to diseases like syphilis and tuberculosis, not to mention diseases like mumps and measles that we shrug off as childhood illnesses." Meanwhile, writes historian R.D.K. Herman, American missionaries wrote off diseases as being the fault of Native Hawaiians' dress, parenting, religion, or immorality.

Another disease that wreaked havoc among Native Hawaiians was Hansen's disease. Known as leprosy at the time, it disproportionately affected Native Hawaiians. People with Hansen's disease were shunned and forced to live in remote leper colonies. Herman notes that public worries about leprosy were used to cast Native Hawaiians as unclean and unhealthy, just as wealthy American interests were trying to cast the Hawaiian monarchy from their country.

These narratives helped white missionaries and plantation owners justify their control of the islands. During the 19th century, they turned Hawaii from a Native stronghold into a missionary-controlled plantation colony.

By 1920, there were fewer than 24,000 Native Hawaiians left in Hawaii. Today, Native Hawaiians face significant health disparities according to the Centers for Disease Control and Prevention. Despite those challenges, the Native Hawaiian population is on the rise. By 2060, there are projected to be more than 500,000 Native Hawaiians in Hawaii, in part due to higher fertility rates. But those growing numbers can't undo the devastating effects of the infectious diseases settlers brought to the Hawaiian islands—diseases that changed the very fabric of Native Hawaiian society forever.

SITE 6:

KONA INN

Many years ago, Papa ' Ula (papa = flat, ula`ula = red, red flats), was an area that contained a heiau built under Chief Umi, a ruling chief of Hawaii Island. This heiau was used as a temple of human sacrifice as recently as the 15th century. This is today where the historically famous Kona Inn Shopping Village is located.

First hand eyewitness accounts by Inn security guards have revealed that the Inn has had its fair share of unexplained events. Radios are reported to turn on and off by themselves, tools move on their own and employees at a restaurant report multiple instances of paranormal activity after hours when just a few people are around.

The Kona Inn was built in 1928 by the Inter-Island Steam Navigation Company and during its heyday had 20 rooms booked solid for steamer passengers. With its saltwater swimming pool, tennis courts and cocktail lounge, it offered wealthy Kona residents the amenities of a country club.

Responsible for the start of commercial tourism in the Kailua Kona area, the Kona Inn was built by Charles Dickey, an architect who created many of the state's impressive buildings. There was no-county water in Kailua until 1953 so the Kona Inn acquired a water system from an abandoned sugar mill. It piped water to the hotel and manager's quarters.

The 2-story structure, carefully designed to blend with the palm fringed Kona shore, found its 20 rooms booked solidly for months in advance. The Kona Inn became Hawaii's favorite refuge for kamaainas as well as the world traveler. The new hostelry was responsible for the popularity of the colorful Kona Coast.

The Inn was also instrumental in developing the Kona Coast as one of the world's greatest fishing areas. With the Inn as unofficial billfish tournament headquarters, the place has attracted marlin fishermen from all over the globe. Despite the passage of time and pressures of growth, the Kona Inn still blends in harmony with its environment. The nostalgia of the past is an important factor in the Kona Inns lasting popularity.

The Kona Inn had its last overnight guest in 1976. Today, it is home to the sprawling Kona Inn Shopping Village and Kona Inn Restaurant. In 2008, the Kona Inn celebrated its 80th year as a historical landmark to all the visitors and residents on the beautiful Kona Coast, situated where it's always been, right on the waterfront in the heart of town, offering one of the most beautiful restaurant settings in the world. The open air environment with unobstructed views of the Kona sunsets offers a once-in-a-lifetime opportunity for a romantic dinner accompanied by the wonderful sounds of waves breaking right in front of the restaurant.

The Inn was considered to be a pioneering effort in the neighbor island hotel industry. Previous to the Kona Inn, the passengers aboard the company steamers had only haphazard room arrangements at outlying stops. An editorial in the Honolulu Star-Bulletin Feb. 7, 1928 summed up the enthusiasm of the new venture:

"The land of the first Kamehameha; the land which cradled the old Federation of the Hawaiian Islands; the storied land where an English ship's captain was worshipped before natives found him human and slew him there, is to be opened at last to the comfort-loving tourists of the world. Soon after the completion of the hotel, the territory will have cause to be grateful to the foresight and enterprise of Inter-Island."

–Honolulu Star Bulletin, 1928.

Credit for the distinctive style of Hawaiian architecture goes to Charles William "C. W." Dickey (1871-1942). His initial designs in Hawaii were eclectic to say the least. He felt a strong need to adapt his buildings to the local environment. Such was the case for his designs for the hotel at the edge of Kilauea Volcano known as Volcano House and the Kona Inn. At the center of the Kona Inn Shopping Village, which stands out from the rest of the inn, is the "Lava Lookout Tower" and is of Richardsonian Romanesque style of architecture.

For those who experience getting stuck in traffic in the Kona area today, just imagine what it was like years ago, before Kona became a resort destination. Visitors would travel approximately 121 miles from Hilo through Volcano in an estimated 14 hours. The return trip (estimated 9 hours) would be a 97 mile "short cut" to Hilo via Waimea and Hamakua Coast, with a spare tire and patch kit that is. The roads were unforgiving because of sharp lava, deep gulches and steep slopes and many travelers found out the hard way.

BONUS:

52 SUPERNATURAL PLACES ON HAWAII ISLAND

Originally written for 52 Perfect Days

http://www.52perfectdays.com/travel-tips/52-supernatural-places-Hawaii-island/

1) **Hulihe'e Palace** – Numerous sightings have taken place at Hulihe'e Palace in Kona. Visitors have reported witnessing a child ghost, possibly the young son of King Kamehameha III, Prince Albert, as well as the ghost of Princess Ka'iulani. A recent sighting during a ghost tour of a lady in a white gown occurred at the Palace, leading some to believe there are still spirits wandering the grounds.

2) **Hilo Memorial ("Crying Babies", "Babies Cry")** – In an old hospital in Kaumana, Hilo, the hallways of an old burned down hospital sometimes resound with distant, surreal cries. Years ago, a fire scorched the hospital nursery and there were many victims. The shell of the old hospital building still stands, as do the restless souls of the poor victims who still haunt it to this day. Visit Kahuna Research Group online to read

my investigation report from a previous visit to this location.

3) **King Kamehameha Kona Beach Hotel** – Local legend claims that the top floor of this hotel is haunted. People have reported hearing footsteps, chanting, and battle cries. Some even claim to see ancient Hawaiian warrior apparitions. The reason for this haunting seems lie in the fact that this area is where King Kamehameha lived out the end of his life. On the bottom floor of the hotel, in the gallery, there are a row of oil paintings, one being a rendering of Queen Liliuokalani. The unsmiling picture appears to breathe in and out while glaring; leading some to believe the painting itself is haunted.

4) **Saddle Road** – Saddle Road is known for its fair share of the supernatural. Similar to Oahu's "Pork over the Pali" story, legend says if you carry pork over Saddle Road, now called Daniel K. Inouye Highway, your car may break down or you might experience something supernatural. Some people on the island think that if you see a young girl, especially if she is wearing a red dress, it is the spirit of Pele, the goddess of the volcano. People say they have seen a lone

hitchhiker on Saddle Road. Legend says if you see her, you should always pick her up.

5) **MacKenzie State Park** – MacKenzie State Park, located in Opihikao on the scenic Red Road in Puna, is said to be one of the most haunted places on the Big Island. It has a slightly checkered history, including unsolved murders and reports of Night marchers. For years, local residents have reported seeing ghosts or experiencing strange unearthly phenomena, some of these occurrences even happening in broad daylight! People who take pictures at the park are sometimes baffled at mysterious objects appearing out of nowhere in some of the shots, including me! Local fishermen who fish at night have witnessed mysterious iridescent fireballs that bounce and roll along the surf and then disappear into the sea caves. Overnight campers have also reported seeing similar flickering green fires dancing around the park. Visit KahunaResearchGroup.org and search for MacKenzie for my detailed supernatural investigation report from MacKenzie State Park.

6) **Pu'uhonua o Honaunau** – A place of refuge. Anyone breaking the ancient Hawaiian laws, the Kapu

(taboo), was usually put to death. However, if the culprit could reach a city of refuge before being killed, he or she could work off their misdeeds there. It is said that the ghosts of some poor souls who never made it inside are still trying to make it into the sanctuary. Reports of sightings at this site vary from a 30ft tall specter that walks on water, to a traveling ball of light that moves throughout the park.

7) **Mauna Kea** – The Big Island's strongest vortex and most sacred cultural site, also the tallest mountain on earth measured from the sea floor to the summit. For centuries, Hawaiian royalty have been buried on the slopes of this mountain and it is unknown how many burial sites there really are. Listed in the Hawaii Vortex Field Guide as the strongest vortex on the Big Island, the area has an intense natural energy that makes it a hotspot for reports of supernatural sightings, such as UFO's, "cloud ships", and strange fireballs, known locally as the akualele.

8) **Naha Stone** - In 1775 Kamehameha proved his strength and power by overturning the Naha stone which weighed nearly five thousand pounds. According to prophecy, anyone who turned over the

Naha stone would conquer all of the islands. Today the Naha stone rests in front of the Hawaii County Library in Hilo near the site of an ancient heiau.

9) **Pu'ukohola Heiau (Hill of the Whale)** – This heiau is said to receive its mysterious power from a natural spring at the base of the hill, which could contribute to the many sightings that have taken place here. In order to become king and unite all the islands in Hawaii, Chieftain Kamehameha was instructed by the prophet Kapoukahi to build a temple in honor of the war god Ku. Completed in 1791, Pu'ukohola Heiau was erected expressly for ceremonies related to war. The temple is said to be heavily haunted by those who were victims of human sacrifice.

10) **Kona Lagoon Resort** - The Kona Lagoon was torn down in 2004 after sitting vacant since 1988. The story behind the demise of the hotel was that the hotel itself was haunted. A story from the Honolulu Advertiser called it cursed. "Surrounded by ancient temples and archaeological sites, it was built on the dwelling place of supernatural twin sisters, who took the form of lizards, according to Hawaiian legend.

11) **Royal Kona Inn** – The Royal Kona Inn sits on the ancient King's Trail, where ghostly Night Marchers are said to march to and from battle. A report by a previous guest at the Inn stated they woke up in the middle of the night and felt as if they were being choked; a common report as far as supernatural Hawaii goes. Based on the advice of a local, the bed was moved out of the pathway and the incident was never reported to happen again.

12) **Reports of the Night Marchers** - Night Marchers are ghostly apparitions of a band of beings who move with purpose to the beat of pounding drums. Some say they are armed spirit warriors marching to or from battle, carrying ancestral weaponry and clothed in decorated helmets and cloaks. Other accounts tell of high-ranking Ali'i (ruler) spirits being guided to places of high importance, or to welcome new warriors to join in battle. The legend of the Night Marchers was born when Hawaii's pre-Tahitian inhabitants were spotted descending the mountains where they lived in order to avoid slaughter by the invading Tahitians. This is oral history recorded in the book, "Tales from the Night Rainbow".

13) Mauna Loa - This 13,680-foot-tall mountain is home to the Hawaiian goddess of fire, Madame Pele. Rumblings within the volcanoes on the islands are said to drive her out to warn people of impending eruptions. Reports of sightings of Pele span over two centuries. Her spirit appears along forest roads or in other public places. Although her age varies, she is always wearing a red muumuu and is usually accompanied by a small white dog. Two ruined heiau platforms, one at Uwekahuna Bluff and the other on Waldron Ledge, are said to contain spiritual imprints dating back to the times when human sacrifices were made to Pele.

14) Ola'a Boy in the Pond – There is a village on the Big Island known as 'Ola'a. In 1947 a gang of neighborhood kids were playing on the shore of a local pond when one of them, named Tanaka, fell in and drowned. When they found the boy's body, he was at the very bottom of the pond, sitting calmly upon a rock with his arms by his side, his eyes and mouth wide open. People have reported being tugged by some unseen force near this pond. Nowadays children are warned to avoid the pond, for fear of being pulled in.

15) Uncle Billie's Hilo Bay Hotel – An online review from July 27, 2010 by a previous guest reports a pretty startling experience. According to the person, a fisherman, he was awoken in the dead of night by the feeling of his blanket being tugged off. A ghostly apparition of a lady was standing at the end of his bed, materialized only from the knees up. He left the hotel immediately and spent the night on his boat, never to go back.

16) Mo'okini Heiau - Mo'okini Heiau was for centuries the most important temple in the Big Island district of Kohala and much of its history has come to the present through oral tradition. The original temple was built near the end of the first millennium by Mo'okini, a local priest. It was subsequently rebuilt and enlarged, circa 1370, by Pa'ao, a priest who arrived from the south Pacific, bringing with him new gods, and the tradition of human sacrifice, a practice that endured for centuries after his death. Reports of the number of sacrifices range from hundreds to tens of the thousands, leaving a huge imprint of energy in the area.

17) Naniloa Hotel - Naniloa Hotel sits on the site of an old Hawaiian burial ground, and allegedly a night clerk at next door's country club had a firsthand view from his desk of night spirits trolling the hallways and outside area of the Naniloa. Reports say the apparitions were amazing and that they defied the laws of physics. This story is well known with locals on the Big Island. Also, sightings of an Edwardian-era lady who walks the area have been reported by local fisherman.

18) **U.H. Hilo – Hale Kanilehua, Eerie Dorm** - It was said that a house once stood where the dorm is now. During the demolition of the house, a boy was playing in the area and died. On the girl's side of dorm, the little boy was sighted on the ground floor. Sounds of the little boy walking up and down the hall, sounds of him talking and laughing, and the sound of his ball bouncing down the hall can be heard. There is a sound of whistling wind whipping through an unoccupied room, almost sounding like that of someone in agony, the feeling of being watched, toilets flushing by themselves, water turning on and off by themselves, things being moved, and sound of someone walking up and down hallway.

19) Hilo Hawaiian Hotel - The Hilo bay front has been hit by numerous tsunamis, two of the most devastating happened in 1946 and 1960. A guest at the Hilo Hawaiian Hotel writes that they were awoken one night by bright lights bouncing around the room despite having a room facing the bay. The second night, the same guest asked that only "good spirits" visit them, and they awoke to find an apparition of a middle-aged gentleman wearing 18th century period clothing in the doorway.

20) Hilo's Haunted House – In Hilo, at the corner of Kilauea and Lanikaula Streets, a house once stood where strange things happened. Sightings of a 7- to 8- foot tall manly figure have been reported to occur here near sundown. Looking neither to the right nor to the left, saying nothing to anyone, he walks right off into the bushes and disappears. Whether the giant figure of a man is still seen in Hilo is unknown.

21) Aston Kona by the Sea – A couple was staying at the Aston Kona Inn (now called Aston Kona by The Sea) and on the first night one of the couple awoke in the dark for no reason. They looked at the room clock. It was 4:04 A.M. The following night, they awoke again.

The alarm clock said it was 4:04 A.M. The last night they were there one person woke up again for no apparent reason. They were scared to look at the alarm clock but felt compelled...and it said 4:04 A.M. Maybe something happened there at 4:04 A.M. It's hard to say for sure...but this report really makes you wonder!

22) **Sheraton Kona** – Employees at this resort say there are two little girls that play in the hallway of the hotel where the guest rooms are located. The guests reportedly call security to tell them to stop, but the security guard has been getting that phone call for years and knows there is nothing he can do, as the girls are just ghosts. Others report a man that stands at the cliff in front of the hotel from time to time. He just disappears when you look away and then back again.

23) **Captain Cook** - In the day the locals in Captain Cook, Hawaii do their thing exactly like anywhere other, but tormented ghosts of the past in this settlement don't appear to be determined to pack up and leave. Nighttime is un-departed time around here. This is the area where Captain Cook was killed in battle. Folks who have never stayed for the night in this settlement

may not be convinced of its superstitious history, but a stay here make anybody a believer.

24) Kona's mermaid – If you're ever in Kona, and you are looking to do some diving, chances are you will come across Jack's Diving Locker. The diving company's logo features a mermaid, and according to their website, the logo was inspired from a real mermaid sighting by one of their boat's captain.

25) Heiau of the Mermaid – On the road to Ho'okena, near the ocean, there is a special heiau that not many people know about. One night, near this heiau, a witness reported seeing a golden glow forming into a small girl, who then disappeared beneath the waves in a mermaid-like fashion. Reports surfaced that the land's former steward was sworn to secrecy regarding the heiau unless someone had a mystical experience there, being able to recall certain details, which the eye-witness did. Three different sightings of mermaids in this area have been reported.

26) Kilauea Volcano - Kilauea volcano is the scene of many Pele sightings. Many people, residents and visitors alike, leave offerings to her, some to the dismay of park officials who clean up broken glass bottles of gin each year. Reports of Pele sightings are common on all islands; however most sightings occur at her home, the volcano. If you are lucky enough to see Pele, consider it a blessing. Just make sure you don't take any lava or sand off island, or you might be seeing her again soon.

27) Pele's Curse - Pele's Curse is the belief that anything natively Hawaiian, such as sand, rock, or pumice, will impart bad luck on whoever takes it away from the island. One version about the legend's genesis is this: a disgruntled park ranger, angry at the number of rocks that were being taken from the islands by visitors, said that Pele would curse them with bad luck should they take anything. Another version often told is that bus drivers, tired of the dirt and grime brought on their buses by the tourists' collection of rocks, started the story at the beginning of each tour to discourage the rock collecting. True or not, every year countless tourists send these back in order to escape the awful bad luck they acquired.

28) Laupahoehoe – It is said this small town is governed by the spirits of days gone by. Cabinets dance around, words come from the night, spirits call your name. Laupahoehoe (leaf of lava) is known for what happened on April 1st, 1946, the April fool's tsunami, when three towering tidal waves roared over the peninsula killing many residents including over 20 children and four teachers. Other than one mangled body (crushed by the rocks) the others were never found. Only two children and one teacher survived and today a memorial stands in remembrance of the lives lost.

29) Laupahoehoe Railway Museum – Between 1909 and 1913, the Hamakua Division of the railroad was constructed to service the sugar mills north of Hilo. Early in the morning of April 1, 1946, a massive tsunami struck several low-lying areas of the Big Island. The railroad line between Hilo and Pa'auilo suffered massive damage; bridges collapsed, trestles tumbled, and one engine was literally swept off the tracks. The museum claims to have a collection of rail photographs that show a series of strange apparitions from a time when double exposure was not well known. Today, employees report hearing footsteps and background music playing softly.

30) Palace Theater - The Palace Theater is said to be one of our local haunts. Built in 1925, it is one of the more prominent public buildings constructed in Hilo in the early 20th century. It was restored years ago after having been closed and is now open. The projector room is said to have two spirits who still operate the machine from time to time. An employee reported when she first began working the projector, the activity was more prominent, but as time went on, and she became comfortable talking to the spirits, activity ceased. Another witness claims to have been touched by a spirit on her shoulder by a tall male entity.

31) Ke'ei Beach – Sightings of warrior apparitions have been reported at Ke'ei beach on the Big Island. According to an eyewitness, the apparitions were fighting with war clubs just outside of their house. Apparently a battle was fought on these grounds in the ancient past and it was Pokane night the night of the sighting. Another witness reports feeling strange at times while at the beach and seeing a black figure roaming around near sundown. Both eye-witnesses refuse to return after dark.

32) Kealakehe High School – According to Wikipedia,

the name Kealakehe means "the pathway of death" in the Hawaiian language. Numerous sightings have been reported at this Kona School, such as doors opening and closing on their own, witnessed by both students and teachers.

33) **Kohala's Laughing Children** - One night a girl snuck away from her friend's house in Kohala where she was staying for a week to go up the street and meet some boys. On the way she passed a local graveyard when she began to hear voices behind her, but no one was there. The voices grew in to children's laughter, getting louder and louder, scaring the girl who ran back to her friend's house. The friend's Mom told the girl that over 100 years ago there used to be an orphanage across from the graveyard that burned down and several children died in the fire.

34) **South Point** – South Point, the most southern tip of the Big Island, is said to be like a rift in time. Sightings of UFOs and other strange occurrences abound in this area, prompting more than numerous authors to write about the subject. I included South Point in the Hawaii Vortex Field Guide because of the strong energy that is present here, and because a "ley-line"

passes through the area. Just off the southern tip, fisherman report that electronics malfunction on a regular basis and one person even reported to me personally that their boat mysteriously broke down and started leaking while out at sea resulting in having to be rescued by authorities. Ancient ruins can also be found in the area.

35) **Kalapana's Calling Ghost** – A boy named Kalani was walking in Kalapana one day when he heard his name being called from behind a bush. Half expecting it to be a friend playing a trick on him, he was surprised to see it was a beautiful Hawaiian girl calling out to him, "Kalani", Kalani". He followed the voice to a clearing in the woods when he felt the air between him and the girl become noticeably colder, in the middle of a hot day. He ran away when the girl's voice turned violent, almost demon-like, calling his name "KALANI! COME HERE!" A subsequent visit showed that if Kalani would have ventured towards the girl any further he would have fallen into a deep lava pit that was concealed by thick vegetation. His aumakua are said to have put the cold air between him and the girl, preventing him from falling into the pit, scaring him and saving his life.

36) Kuamoʻo Burials – Kuamoʻo Burial Grounds, also known as Lekeleke Burial grounds, was the site of a major battle that ended the old ways of Hawaiian kapu religious system. Located at the southern end of Aliʻi Drive in Kona, the area is checkered with burial mounds and grave markers. Unlike most Hawaiian battles, this one was fought using modern weaponry, including rifles and cannons. A nice place to hike during daylight hours, the scenic area turns eerie once the sun goes down. Chicken skin can be felt here as soon as you pull up in your car. The energy imprint of the area is so intense it once caused my entire investigation team to mysteriously get a taste of blood in our mouths…not to mention our equipment malfunctioned too. The cliffs here can be dangerous, especially during high surf. During our first visit, a hiker accidentally fell over the cliff and had to be rescued.

37) Castle Ruins – Downtown Kona is very historical, with buildings dating back hundreds of years. Some of the history behind these buildings has been lost over the decades. By Kalani Street in Kona, close to MacDonald's, there are ruins of an old building that looks like an old castle, overgrown with vegetation and barely visible from the road. Two friends were visiting the area when one of them claimed their hand was pushed by an invisible force, causing him to drop and break his camera. Afterwards, the friend was also pushed by an unseen force, causing them both to run in fear. They later learned that a king and queen had possibly died there, but that portion of this story is unconfirmed.

38) **Manuka State Wayside Park** - Nicknamed Obake Park, Manuka State Wayside is a small park in south Kona. Next to the parking lot are two graves, each marked by a single gravestone, by now the names well worn and weathered. It is unknown who these graves belong to, but they do exist. One eyewitness learned the hard way that if you camp overnight there you should leave a food offering near the graves otherwise you might be visited by otherworldly beings.

39) **Palani Rd. Sighting** - There is a story of a woman who died in car crash sometime in the 1950's, driving up Palani Road from Kailua-Kona town. It was a rainy, moonless night and the roads were very slick. One curve is particularly bad as you come around it, the road almost hairpins to the left. The woman was

very upset because she caught her lover with another woman. She was crying, and going too fast when her car slid out of control and hit the tree head on. Ever since then, there have been a multitude of accidents - all of the drivers that have run into the exact tree have claimed to have seen a woman, soaking wet and crying, standing in the middle of the road. The drivers claim that while trying to avoid her, they crashed into the tree.

40) **Tombstone of Miloli'i** – A husband and wife couple were on a beach near the village when the husband jumped on what he thought was a flat rock but was actually an old gravestone that had washed away now lying on the beach. As soon as he landed on the stone, he was hit with a tremendous force comparable to being hit from behind with a two-by-four. His wife witnessed the event. When they inspected the stone on the beach they realized it was a tombstone so they notified a villager who had the spooky gravestone returned to its rightful place.

41) **King's Trail** - King's Trail is an old coastal rock trail built by King Kamehameha I who ruled the Hawaiian Islands from 1795 to 1819. This trail circled the entire

Big Island and, for many decades, served as a major travelling route for native Hawaiians to go from one end of the island to the other. Local legends say that the ghosts of ancient Hawaiian warriors are still using this trail. Over the years, people have witnessed eerie sights like a procession of disembodied flickering torches or heard haunting sounds of drumming, chanting and battle cries. These occurrences often happen during a windy rainstorm or on calm moonlit nights.

42) **Ghosts of Greenbank** – Greenbank was a mansion built in North Kohala by Dr. and Mrs. James Wight of Australia. Greenbank has over 100 years of recorded spiritual encounters. Some of the first concerns about the mansion arose when it was to be built upon the same location as an ancient Hawaiian heiau. Another major concern was the fact that Dr. Wight intentionally ignored warnings from local kahunas when he built the home directly over a young girl's grave. Topping the situation off came when he decided to place an extremely evil stone at the base of his veranda, leading to years of illness and misfortune. The strange activity stopped once the stone was donated to the Bishop Museum, where it sits today.

43) Keaau Burial Grounds – A family living in the Hawaiian Paradise Park area of Keaau reported strange activity happening in their home after a recent remodel, a common occurrence in reports of supernatural activity. Loud banging in a particular bedroom was reported by three different family members at three different times. They learned that an ancient burial ground was really close to their home which they felt was cause of the strange happenings. The family reported the activity to be steadily getting worse, and they are actively seeking someone to bless their home.

44) Keauhou Area – Reports of activity are constantly reported in the Keauhou area. Between the numerous burials in the area and the hotels built on sacred ground, Keauhou in general is known locally as one of the Island's most haunted areas. One story tells of a lady who took a stone from the beach, possibly near an ancient heiau, back to her hotel room. She had a vivid dream of a Hawaiian warrior with a traditional weapon telling her to put the stone back right away. The next day the lady took the stone back, but on the way, along the trail, she claims to have seen the same warrior apparition walking with her.

Ghost Towns of the Big Island

A **ghost town** is an abandoned village, town or city, usually one which contains substantial visible remains. A town often becomes a ghost town because the economic activity that supported it has failed, or due to natural or human-caused disasters such as floods, government actions, uncontrolled lawlessness, war, or lava flows.

45) **Honu'apo** - Now a State Park called Whittington Park. Take Hwy 11 on the southeast side of the island and it can be found between Pahala and Naalehu. Honu'apo (turtle cove) was a thriving 1883 port town with industrial warehouses, a mill, and railroad connection. The port was used to transport taro and sugarcane grown to the town area. When the roads were improved, all shipments went by truck and the residents deserted the town. The pier was rebuilt twice after tsunamis had destroyed it. After the second tsunami, they gave up on rebuilding the pier and it was allowed to decay.

46) **Kapoho** - Kapoho was a farming town, it had stores, a church, school, several houses, but was destroyed by the 1960 lava flow, much the same way as Kalapana 30

years later. From Hilo take Hwy 11 to Keaau. Turn on 130, proceed 11 miles to Pahoa. Turn on route 132. About 6 miles down the road, on the left, is a forest of ironwood trees growing in red cinders in front of a small (100') red rock volcano. This is where the town was.

47) **Kalapana** - Kalapana was one of the most beautiful old Hawaiian villages on the island. A lava flow struck the area in 1986 and destroyed 181 homes, a visitor center and maintenance shop in Hawaii Volcanoes National Park, highways, and treasured historical/archeological sites. The famous painted church was moved to a new location but the community center was destroyed. A few die-hard residents continue to live near area, still facing active lava flows.

Leaping Places of the Soul

[Author's note: Many of these portals were reported in the book "Hawaiian Mythology" by Martha Warren Beckwith in 1940. Beckwith utilized numerous texts, which are today rare or hard to obtain, to construct her study.]

In Hawaiian mythology, when your body dies, it is believed your soul begins a journey towards a leaping place of the soul believed to be a portal to the Other World. The worst fate that can befall a soul is to be abandoned by its god and left to stray, a wandering spirit in some barren and desolate place, feeding upon spiders and night moths. Such spirits are believed to be malicious and to take delight in leading travelers astray; hence the wild places they haunt on each island. While there is typically one or two leaping places per island, such as Ka'ena point on Oahu, on the Big Island there are said to be at least five, nearly one leina for each district.

48) Kukui-o-pae – Kohala District - Very near the northwestern extremity of the Kohala district, most northern point of Hawaii Island, near Upolu Point and less than three miles from mysterious Mo'okini Heiau and also the birthplace of King Kamehameha I.

49) Waipi'o Valley – Hamakua District - Entrance is at a cleft on a high bluff overlooking the sea or possibly on the edge of a valley wall, or mouth of a river and a tree usually serves as the roadway by which the soul takes its departure. The Waipi'o entryway is said to be at the mouth of the valley at a place called "Keoni", an area long ago covered by sand to conceal it from human eyes.

50) Maka-hana-loa – Hilo District – Retained by Lunalilo at the Māhele. "Cape and land division...an ancient leaping place for souls. A sacred bamboo grove called Hō-mai-ka-'ohe (hand me the bamboo) was planted here by the god Kāne; bamboo knives used for circumcision came from this grove." The cape is not identified but may be the one now known as "Pepeekeo Point", which is far from the land of Pepeekeo.

51) Kumu-kahi – Puna District – Cape Kumukahi is the easternmost point of the Big Island. The name means "First Beginnings", and it was named after a hero of the Kahiki who landed here. Kahiki means "east", or "where the sun rises". Legend has it that the 4 wives of Kumukahi, represented by volcanic pillars along the coast, tossed the sun back and forth. This is suggestive of the movement of the sun between the solstices as it moves along the horizon. In addition, the nearby Kukii Heiau is an ancient temple which served as a navigational school, built in the ancient times, and rebuilt in the 16th Century. The Cape Kumukahi Light is a lighthouse on the easternmost point of Hawaii. It is best known for its survival through an eruption of Kilauea in 1960.

52) Leina-akua – Ka'u District – Leina-akua translates to "God-leap". Hawaiian scholar Mary Kawena Puku'i recorded that an old kukui tree in Ka'u was used to "cast-off" spirits into the otherworld.

Mahalo for coming with us to paranormal paradise! We hope you enjoyed your visit and the stories you heard! Please be sure to leave us a review on TripAdvisor or Google. *Aloha & Mahalo!!!*

ABOUT THE AUTHOR

Zach Royer is an author & publisher from the Pacific Northwest with a passion for the environment, world travel, ancient history and modern mystery.

In 2011, he moved to Hawai'i where he followed spirit and created Kahuna Research Group, Hawaii's premier paranormal research organization who continues to be at the forefront of exploring Hawaii's secrets & mysteries, including lost pyramids, healing vortexes, Mu/Lemuria, UFO sightings and much more. In 2015 he created Big Island Ghost Tours as a way to keep the ancient stories and legends alive.

He is the author of *Pyramid Rising: Planetary Acupuncture to Combat Climate Change* (2012), the *Hawai'i Vortex Field Guide* (2014), the *Kona Haunted Hele Guidebook* (2015) and the *Maui Vortex Field Guide* (2019). He is presently working on his next book, the *Oahu Vortex Field Guide*, book three of the four-part "Island Vortex Series" from KRG Publishing.

Zach lives in Kailua Kona and is involved in many cool projects, frequently traveling around the world to lead vortex retreats and other unique workshops & adventures. Follow Zach on Instagram **@zachroyer_** and at www.ZachRoyer.com to see what adventures he is planning next!

Web design, products & more at ZOAT.services

2022 Sponsored Page Rate

Sponsor your business with a like-minded publishing company.

Limited space available!

KRG Publishing

FULL PAGE

4.5" X 7.5"

~~$250~~

$200

*Price displayed is for our 3 month quarterly rate.

Learn more or purchase a sponsorship at www.KahunaResearchGroup.org/advertising

Made in the USA
Middletown, DE
03 June 2022

66607960R00050